TENNYSON

AN OCCULTIST AS HIS WRITINGS PROVE

(1920)

A. P. Sinnett

ISBN 0-7661-0280-7

Request our FREE CATALOG of over 1,000
Rare Esoteric Books
Unavailable Elsewhere

Freemasonry * Akashic * Alchemy * Alternative Health * Ancient Civilizations * Anthroposophy * Astral * Astrology * Astronomy * Aura * Bacon, Francis * Bible Study * Blavatsky * Boehme * Cabalah * Cartomancy * Chakras * Clairvoyance * Comparative Religions * Divination * Druids * Eastern Thought * Egyptology * Esoterism * Essenes * Etheric * Extrasensory Perception * Gnosis * Gnosticism * Golden Dawn * Great White Brotherhood * Hermetics * Kabalah * Karma * Knights Templar * Kundalini * Magic * Meditation * Mediumship * Mesmerism * Metaphysics * Mithraism * Mystery Schools * Mysticism * Mythology * Numerology * Occultism * Palmistry * Pantheism * Paracelsus * Parapsychology * Philosophy * Plotinus * Prosperity & Success * Psychokinesis * Psychology * Pyramids * Qabalah * Reincarnation * Rosicrucian * Sacred Geometry * Secret Rituals * Secret Societies * Spiritism * Symbolism * Tarot * Telepathy * Theosophy * Transcendentalism * Upanishads * Vedanta * Wisdom * Yoga * *Plus Much More!*

Kessinger Publishing, LLC
P.O. Box 160, Kila, MT 59920 U.S.A.
Phone (406) 756-0167 Fax (406) 257-5051
http://www.kessingerpub.com
email: books@kessingerpub.com

TENNYSON
AN OCCULTIST
AS HIS WRITINGS PROVE

By
A. P. SINNETT
Author of
"The Occult World," "Esoteric Buddhism,"
"The Growth of the Soul," "In the Next World,"
etc., etc., etc.

LONDON
THEOSOPHICAL PUBLISHING HOUSE
1 Upper Woburn Place, W.C.1
1920

CONTENTS

CHAPTER		PAGE
I	Introduction	1
II	Tennyson, the Genius	11
III	Tennyson, the Occultist	45

TENNYSON AN OCCULTIST

CHAPTER I

INTRODUCTION

THE world at large only learned by degrees to appreciate Tennyson's poetry. It was rudely received at first, but gradually its beauty, its sympathy with human emotion, and, as time went on, its wide range and variety, taught us all to realise that a very great poet had taken birth amongst us. Its beauty throughout must appeal to all who have ears for the music of verse in union with intensity of feeling, and delicacy of expression. But some of us in recent years—profiting by current disclosure of much natural truth previously hidden from generations unripe to receive it—have been deeply impressed by unmistakable evidence in some of Tennyson's earlier and many of his later poems, showing that he had already acquired a deep insight into superphysical science, that he must have been in conscious touch with

Beings evolved far beyond the stage of progress reached by ordinary humanity, that he was, in fact, an Occultist in advance of his time.

To establish this by reference to veiled hints that the ordinary reader passes over, without understanding them, is the main purpose of the present little volume, and the interpretation that can now be applied to some verses that will be quoted, is so obviously the right one, that, in the familiar phrase, it will leap to the eyes of everyone acquainted with the growing body of knowledge relating to the loftier mysteries of Nature that has accumulated on our hands in connexion with the progress of the Theosophical Movement. But Tennyson lived and wrote at a period when none of this knowledge had become available for public use. As we see now—quotations from his writings will show this not as a matter of opinion, but as a fact—Tennyson was individually put into touch with teachers on a level far above that of ordinary humanity, he came by personal experience to know that he—the real entity known as Tennyson to himself and others—could pass out of the body, take cognisance of realms around unperceived by the physical senses, receive instruction there from Beings far advanced beyond ordinary human conditions, and (this was his all important capacity) bring back the recollection of what he had thus learned to his physical brain when he returned to the body. In these days all this—for a considerable number of theosophical

INTRODUCTION

students — has become completely intelligible; for some in turn a matter of personal experience. But in Tennyson's time what would have been thought of him, by even his most devoted admirers, if he had frankly said, for example, "When out of the body last night on the Astral plane I was shown by certain members of the Divine Hierarchy such or such scenes from the early history—the Akasic records—of the Solar System." That genius and madness were nearly allied would have been the only possible conclusion for his hearers at that date. He could only indulge his inner consciousness by writing something to that effect in language no one of his period could possibly understand. That he did this pretty frequently it will be my purpose to show.

But Tennyson as the Occultist will be better understood if we first consider all that is implied when we speak of him as a genius. For most people the term has no definite scientific meaning. It merely expresses glowing admiration; has precise value only for those who understand the laws governing human evolution. Thus, before dealing with the occultism in Tennyson's poetry, it may be well worth while to study its broader aspects and to trace the way in which the evolution of his genius led up to his development as an Occultist. However, in dealing with former lives through which he has passed, and the conditions of superphysical existence between each, I must refer readers unfamiliar with the great natural programme of human life to other books for a full explanation of all this—for example, to "The Occult World," "The Growth of the Soul," and "Expanded Theosophical Knowledge" by the present writer. For all genuine students of the subject, the system of rebirth and intervening rest in the Astral world, with the absorption of gathered experience into the permanent consciousness, is as definitely recognised and understood as for the physiologist the system which provides for growth —the circulation of the blood. Those who disbelieve in the fact that human evolution is accomplished by means of reincarnation, show that they have neglected the study of the subject and have no right to form an opinion of that kind. The system cannot be proved in the way we prove the equality of the angles at the base of an isosceles triangle, but it can be proved by the line of reasoning sometimes adopted by Euclid, which culminates in the phrase "which is absurd." The denial of reincarnation leads straight to conclusions of that nature; and as this volume may fall into the hands of many readers who may not have realised the truth of what has just been said, it seems worth while before entering on the study of the poems as they illustrate the great natural law, to explain this sufficiently to dissipate the ill-founded objections continually levelled against it.

The law does *not* contemplate the absorption of

INTRODUCTION

any mature Ego in a newly-born child. The real consciousness of the Ego remains on higher spiritual levels during the childhood of the body destined to be its habitat when *that* is mature. The obvious necessity for the system, as explaining away the terrible inequality of condition in human life, is the first powerful argument for its acceptance. We *know* by an ever-increasing multitude of experiences that the Soul or Ego is an entity which inhabits the body in ordinary waking life: completely retains its individuality, when the body is destroyed, in another vehicle of consciousness; in very many cases is there enabled to remember former incarnations; in many is able to do this while still making use of a physical body. Thus we get utterly free from the idea that each new baby is a fresh creation thrown at random into happy or miserable surroundings in a way that is incompatible with belief in a just God, even if we leave loving kindness out of account. A long series of lives beginning on crude or humble levels and providing for the gradual growth of a Soul by manifold experiences, constitutes a method of natural evolution for each human being that is in harmony with all the other gradual processes of Nature. Sex is accounted for. In the course of its numerous incarnations the Soul is sometimes embodied in the male, sometimes in the female sex. Relationships are not confused in this way. They are completed, but—I am not now concerned with an exhaustive survey of the system and need not follow up that idea.

The specially important aspect of the system to emphasise in connexion with Tennyson's incarnations, has to do with the way it provides for the abnormal growth in special cases, of some particular mental or artistic capacity. In every case growth is accomplished by gathering experience. But few Egos devote equal attention to every kind of capacity. If they are specially attracted at any given stage of their progress through the ages by some one kind of capacity that becomes especially emphasised life after life. In one sense, though subject, of course, to the supreme Divine Will, we are thus our own creators. Some Egos chiefly devote themselves to the cultivation of the scientific capacity and become more and more efficient in that way life after life, till they reach what is commonly called genius in that direction. And great poets are the product of persistent effort in the exercise of the mental and artistic attributes associated with their beautiful aspirations. In these prefatory explanations I am dealing with general principles—I will endeavour to show later how they apply to Tennyson.

But some other general principles must be discussed, before I enter on the task I have undertaken, the interpretation of Tennyson's poetry in a way that will reveal meaning in it that has not hitherto been generally perceived. I am the better able to accomplish this because I have had several recent opportunities of discussing the subject with the great poet himself, now, of course, in life on a higher plane of existence. For very large numbers of people who know, of their own experience, that it is possible to communicate with the other world to which we all pass on when we escape from the imprisonment of flesh, there will be nothing surprising in the statement I have just made. For other large numbers—remaining strangely ignorant of the progress made during the last fifty years in linking the two worlds together—I know what I have said will seem bewildering or incredible. That this should be so, is grotesquely absurd. Nothing in scientific discovery during the last fifty years is a more definite addition to our knowledge than the fact that intercourse between those still in the physical body and those who have passed on, is possible. At first the fact was startling and it soon appeared that methods of communication were imperfect; liable in some cases to lend themselves to imposture, but the broad truth that Spiritualists were in touch with the next plane of existence beyond the physical, became established with overwhelming certainty, however frequently it turned out that the identification of people communicating from the other side was difficult. For reasons that gradually became intelligible "Spirits" were not always what they seemed, but that did not affect the broad certainty that they were speaking from the other side, and in enormous numbers Spiritualists had abundant proof that they were really in touch with friends they had known in this life. The literature of Spiritualism establishing this all-important state of things grew to huge proportions. No one who dives into it with reasonable perseverance can doubt its main contentions.

Then, within the last thirty or forty years further developments ensued. The Theosophical revelation—for it is nothing less—put a scientific face upon all discoveries connected with future life; not merely on the immediate future, but on great vistas of knowledge connected with still more exalted states of consciousness. With these it is not my present purpose to deal, but incidentally the higher occultism, included in Theosophy, in its turn included new methods of dealing with and acquiring knowledge concerning the immediately "next world." This is how it has come to pass that I have had recent conversations with Tennyson in connexion with my efforts, in which he has taken interest, to show that he, in physical life, had touch with those semi-Divine sources of information which I have been privileged also to have touch with ever since my earliest books relating to the subject inaugurated the Theosophical movement in the Western world. For reasons that every genuine occult student will understand, a thin veil must be drawn over the detailed methods of communication available for my use; and the self-sufficient "sceptic" (or ignoramus) who challenges every occult writer to bring him proofs of this or that statement that he cannot accept, fails to understand that it is not worth the while of the occulist to undertake his elementary education. He and many millions are in some respects at all events at a stage of evolution, when they must await the experience of other lives before they can understand superphysical Nature. But in reference to the simple fact that communication between this world and the next is possible, those who honestly want to know the truth have only got to go in search of it, and they will find proofs ready for them in abundance. And very little thought will show them the fatuity of warnings sometimes emanating from blind leaders of the blind to the effect that it is "not intended" we should penetrate mysteries of Nature lying beyond the grave. The ludicrous conceit of those who give such warnings, and in so doing profess to be acquainted with what is, and what is not, Divine intention, would deserve a harsher description, but for its innocent foolishness. Whatever new knowledge we actually acquire is shown by its acquisition to come within the limits of that we are "intended" to have—if we can get it.

So the fact that in the preparation of this little book I have had the advantage of consultation with the Individuality himself whom, in his last life we called Tennyson, will greatly enhance its interest for all—to begin with—who are familiar with such possibilities; as also for others who, provisionally impressed by all I have been saying about those possibilities, may be guided to make a study of the subject. That may easily be done in the present day when the literature of Spiritualism has been enriched by contributions from writers of the highest intellectual rank and the literature of Theosophy—the sequel to Spiritualism—has become equally significant. Meanwhile, apart from that line of thought altogether, I venture to assert in advance that I have proved by the simple evidence of Tennyson's poems as they stand in print, the leading idea I am concerned with emphasising that our great poet was an occultist as well as being a genius.

CHAPTER II

TENNYSON, THE GENIUS

NCE we reach a full comprehension of the natural system by which all Ego consciousness, on humble and exalted levels equally, is enabled to expand, we cannot fail to see in Tennyson a living proof of that system. Whoever endeavours to believe that the baby born in 1809 was a new creation endowed by a capricious Providence with faculties that enabled him to become the greatest poet of the century by the time he was 20, must be content to abandon the idea that things which happen are due to anterior causes. Nor will it do to treat the Will of a capricious Providence as an anterior cause in the case before us. Reverent study of Providential doings or, to use a more definite expression, God's plan in "The Making of Man" shows us gradualness as its leading principle. Oak trees do not flash into existence full grown between night and morning. Sheep and oxen represent ideas developed through æons of natural selection. Great poets or great men of science are the result of protracted efforts in the direction of such greatness, carried on through a long series of earth lives, in

B

each of which the true Ego—or Soul if the word conveys a clearer meaning to the ordinary thinker—is the same all the time, absorbing into its capacity the experience of each life and guided by supreme Divine wisdom and power, into bodies qualified to give expression to the expanded consciousness.

Tennyson was a living illustration of occult teaching concerning human evolution. He was already a poet in childhood, for the simple reason that he was the reincarnation of an Ego that had in previous centuries been manifesting as a great poet over and over again. Advanced occultists know now that in successive lives he was Virgil, Omar Khayyam, Dante and Spenser before he culminated as a greater than any of these—Tennyson. Of course, as soon as the new body began to be available for use, the concentrated poetic capacity gathered from the former lives began to force its way into expression. At eight years old—he tells us himself in some memoranda left for his son and used in the "Memoir" published after his death—he wrote blank verse on a slate, and at 10 or 11 quantities of rhymed verse in the metre Pope employed. Then at Cambridge when 20, he wrote the prize poem "Timbuctoo"; about the same time most of the "Poems by Two Brothers," and in 1830 he gave out the first important volume of his own exclusive work entitled "Poems Chiefly Lyrical."

This collection included two, at least, that already touched the high-water mark of artistic technique—the "Recollections of the Arabian Nights" and "The Day Dream"—then called "The Sleeping Beauty"; also a poem that by some mischance dropped out of notice and was not reprinted in later editions—"The Mystic." It is remarkable as giving the first hint of the author's appreciation of the higher occultism. For the fuller evidence of this we have to look forward to the work of his later life, but "The Mystic" could only have been written by one who felt—without actually knowing—that humanity must include Beings who have risen to loftier heights of spiritual development than are touched by ordinary culture.

The main purpose of the present volume is to show by reference to the poet's published writings that he possessed this knowledge, and a great deal more that clings to it. Furthermore, I want to give my readers the benefit of information concerning the progress of his work that I have been privileged to obtain from him himself during recent years. As I have said already, that statement will excite scornful contempt from the large number of commonplace people around us who are wilfully blind to the immense progress that has been made in these recent years in the development of communications with those who have "passed on." But those who still ridicule the methods and results of ordinary Spiritualism are already left behind by a large and imposing minority who have realised the immense importance of discoveries that have been reached in that way. Others, foolishly clinging to ignorant disbelief, repeat worn-out cries about imposture and delusion. Others again, incapable of denying that Spiritualists get touch with the next world, warn us all off that line of activity, as I have already said, because, they declare, it is *not intended* that we should follow it up. They fail to perceive that this contention involves the insolent assumption that they are in the confidence of God, as to the nature of His plans for human evolution. Clergymen are especially prone to this kind of blasphemy, shameless in regard to their own culpable neglect of opportunities that, properly made use of, might render them a shade less incompetent to play the part of spiritual experts which they unworthily pretend to be.

Meanwhile knowledge expands. From the stage reached by the ordinary Spiritualist—a very important stage though not properly a resting-place—another has been attained to by those who have pushed forward with occult research, and I need not here repeat the contents of many books from my own pen and others which explain the conditions under which some of us have been able to get into touch, not merely with friends who have passed on, but with exponents of lofty wisdom emanating from the Divine Hierarchy.

Profiting by opportunities arising in this way, I have been enabled in connexion with my attempts to show, in review articles and lectures, that Tennyson was truly an occultist, to get into free touch with the great poet himself and to get a good deal more than confirmation of the conclusions I had reached by the simple study of his published writings. He has told me how—in some cases—his occult knowledge was acquired. No mere conventional theory of "genius" would account for that. Much nonsense is often put forward in reference to genius. There is no mystery behind it for those who understand the laws of reincarnation. Roughly it is commonly treated as the exhibition of exalted faculty of art, science or literature where no education or training can account for this. It is simply the fruition of work done in former lives, plus progress made between lives, itself the fruition of aspiration in the one just spent. Tennyson was, in this way, a genius in reference to the exquisite poetry of his early life. He was an occult student under instruction from Beings belonging to the Divine Hierarchy in reference to the definite superphysical knowledge some of the later poems show. And concerning that teaching, I shall have much to say later on—but it is worth while to pause and realise an important idea. The occultist was in his case grafted, so to speak, on the genius. He came into touch with those higher Beings who taught him great truths connected with human evolution, the facts of superhuman history and the principles underlying the laws of evolution which genius alone could never have given him. But it was his genius that made the touch possible.

That last statement needs a little amplification. At a certain stage of human progress habits of exalted thought will naturally put an Ego passing on from physical life in touch with some representative of the Divine Hierarchy, who would convey occult teaching by the usual method of initiation. That would gradually have left him out of the ordinary course of rebirth till he himself became attached to the Divine Hierarchy. But suppose that in some case an Ego has developed extraordinary capacity along some definite line of human activity—art, science or poetry, for example. He may have a predominant desire to perfect himself still further in that department of expression. Then he may forego regular initiation and devote himself, on the higher levels of the Astral world, to the further expansion of his capacity along his chosen line of activity. That may prevent him from any immediate ascent into the ranks of the Divine Hierarchy, but it does not prevent him—as a genius in his own line—from getting conscious touch with that Hierarchy. On the contrary it guarantees him such a touch. And that is how it came to pass that Tennyson becomes at once a genius as a poet, and an instructed pupil of the

"Masters" in reference to the occult laws of human evolution and history.

So, in presuming to think that I can explain him a little better than this has been done by other writers—even though these may have been his warm admirers—I wish first to dwell on the fact, fairly well accepted now, that he was a genius as a poet, in the technical sense that I have assigned to the word above, as well as in the more common meaning of the term—that he was somehow very wonderful in his way.

He must have been studying the art of poetry in each of his inter-incarnate periods from the Virgil life onwards. And his main purpose in each of the later lives seems to have been the improvement of the art of poetry. A leap forward is shown at each stage and the leap from Spenser to Tennyson was the most startling. That is not surprising if we think of progress as gathering momentum all along the line. He has assured me, by the way, that he as Spenser was absolutely the author of "The Faerie Queene." Some Baconians pushing their perfectly well founded belief in Bacon's authorship of the Shakespeare plays and of some other writings with other names attached, have endeavoured to maintain that he was the real author of the poems attributed to Spenser. At the stage of spiritual development Tennyson has reached his memory covers the events of former incarnations and he emphatically declares that as Spenser he wrote every line of the great Elizabethan poem, though he well knew and had much literary consultation with Bacon.

Before going on to examine the full significance of Tennyson's allusions to occult knowledge in his later poems, it will be well to study those of earlier date as illustrating the true character of his genius. His powers of expression were, of course, due in the first instance to the accumulated capacity of his former poetic lives. But his touch on higher planes with Beings belonging to the Divine Hierarchy influenced his writing from the beginning, though probably without being at first comprehended in the waking state. He used to have helpful visions even when at work on the poems published when he was only 20 or 21. And this fact needs a little illumination. The Divine Hierarchy is not a mere aggregation of superhuman Beings all alike. It is specialised in a highly elaborate way. Thus each great department of human activity may be thought of as presided over by a Divine (or at all events highly superhuman) Being devoted to the culture and guidance of incarnate Egos engaged in that particular department of activity or research. Thus there is *a* Being presiding over the scientific progress of this world; inspiring scientific genius; serving out— as it were—fresh discoveries as the growth of civilisation, or the moral development of our race, entitles us to benefit by them. Each scientific genius has become that in exactly the same way that has been traced in Tennyson's case—by the accumulated capacity, the fruit of efforts in former lives. But each, in the new life, may need the stimulus of specific inspiration before it can give rise to new discovery of importance. Moreover, it may sometimes need a check—if brilliant genius unaided starts some too intuitive scientist on a clue to discoveries for which the world is not yet ripe—not morally entitled to enjoy. As in so many other ways, the ordinary humanity of this period is utterly in the dark as to powers and forces operative all around it on planes of activity its present senses do not enable it to perceive.

Though the two fields of activity have little in common, there is a Being of great spiritual exaltation engaged in cultivating the art of poetry. All whose natural capacities flow into that channel come under his watchful care, and I need hardly say that he has long been familiar with the brilliant pupil who, in the life last spent, was incarnated as Tennyson. A time came eventually when all this became clear to the brilliant pupil in question, but his consciousness was impressed by visions given him by the Poetic Master long before he came to understand their origin. Thus in "The Palace of Art" published first in 1832, the wonderful verses describing the pictures on the walls were simply descriptions of what Tennyson had *seen*—pictures that had been shown him in what occultists technically call "the Astral Light." In this connexion the reader may be interested in hearing that once when I myself was trying some mesmeric experiments with a very highly-gifted sensitive I repeated one of the verses in question to see if the words evoked a visible response. Not only did they do so, but the picture called up seemed a living picture, and as my sensitive gazed at it, it underwent changes—melting into new conditions naturally following those dealt with in the poem.

We cannot, by merely tracing the order in which various poems were published, work out any theory concerning the growth of Tennyson's genius. It was in full maturity almost from its earliest manifestation. "The Lady of Shalott," "The Lotus Eaters," and "The Palace of Art" were already in print in the year 1832, when the author was only 24. For sheer beauty of form, subtlety, and tenderness of thought and depth of meaning, those three poems are unrivalled in literature, unsurpassed even by the later work of their author. There is more intensity of emotion in "Locksley Hall," and the "Idylls of the King" have a stately grandeur that cannot be attained by shorter poems. The occult wisdom revealed, though rather closely veiled in still later poems—hardly veiled in "The Ancient Sage"—is not to be looked for in poems which owe their charm, or part of their charm, to exquisite beauty of form; but those which Tennyson's devotees will be best inclined to learn by heart and dream over at leisure are mostly to be found among the early fruits of his dazzling genius, already in mid-day splendour at its dawn. Only by virtue of what we know now concerning the continuity of each individual human life can we account reasonably for this condition of things. Until a very exalted stage of development has been reached the Ego does not remember the external circumstances of former lives, but he does not lose the intellectual or artistic capacities engendered during former lives. We are so used to finding some people dull and stupid and others brilliantly gifted that we either make no effort to understand why that should be so, or else fall back on futile hypotheses concerning heredity. The occult explanation is the only one that can make sense of cases in which splendid capacity is manifested in youth. Tennyson, therefore, to begin with, before he tinged his poetry with occult knowledge, was a living illustration of the laws governing reincarnation. For direct allusion to definite knowledge gained in the current life by what eventually became his conscious touch with the Masters of Wisdom, we must turn to the poems of his later years. The volume containing "The Ancient Sage" was published in 1885, and its inspiration is clearly drawn from the semi-Divine Hierarchy from which the Theosophical Movement derived its original impulse. The author, indeed, must have received much of that inspiration in advance, as many of the poems and fragments of earlier date plainly show. The revelation of occult truth giving rise to the Theosophical Movement only broke upon those who were ready for it, when Tennyson's life was drawing to its close. He was not commissioned to convey the message to the world in clear scientific amplitude. His task seems to have been first to raise the art of poetry to a higher level than it had ever touched before, and then to scatter in advance the fragments of occult truth his latest writings include, to serve a purpose not yet generally understood. They resemble some cryptic hints thrown out by early astronomers who discerned some truths concerning celestial phenomena in advance of their formal scientific discovery. Now that we have, not the complete revelation of occult truth—for that lies beyond the reach of incarnate humanity—but a great volume of it in advance, Tennyson's prophetic hints have a peculiar charm for those of us who can now understand them. For multitudes of his readers the fact that he accepted the leading principles of Theosophic teaching will give that teaching a *prima facie* claim on their attention. For those who have thoroughly absorbed it no collateral guarantees are needed, but there may be many inquiring readers of Theosophical books who will be encouraged at the outset of their study by finding themselves supported by so great and famous a fellow-student as Tennyson.

Before discussing the deep inner meaning of "The Ancient Sage," it is worth while to dwell, as a preparation, on the characteristics of the earlier poems. Foremost among these we have to recognise their supreme beauty of form. If we regard all great leaders of thought or activity as appointed by Divine intention to play some definite part in the evolution of humanity, one may think of Tennyson, as I have already suggested, as charged to raise the art of poetry to a higher level than it had previously reached. This would not have been done by the simple presentation of new thought, however admirable or impressive. It had to be presented in a form worthy of the thought. Beauty of form—of the language in which thought is expressed—needed as much care as the dignity or tenderness of the utterance. Appreciation of beauty is a faculty which grows and expands as human development proceeds. That which is agreeable to the eye of the savage (he has not yet learned to think whether it is beautiful or not) is offensive or ugly in the sight of a civilised man. The savage would not be able to recognise as beautiful that which is so to the civilised man. And as civilisation advances the perception of beauty becomes keener, taste improves—to use a conventional phrase which roughly embodies a profound natural fact. The appreciation of beauty, indeed, is a science that humanity is gradually acquiring. At first the emotion beauty excites seems insulted by exact analysis.

"Oh, to what uses shall we put
　The wild-weed flower that simply blows?
And is there any moral shut
　Within the bosom of the rose?"

But really, capacity to appreciate the rose is going through gradual expansion as the æons roll by. The age of Greek sculpture is but yesterday—identical with our own period—when we contemplate "The Making of Man" as a complete episode in eternity. Beauty expressed in form may touch a higher level; the Greek stage will probably suffice for a long while yet. Beauty as expressed in language has been of later growth. It was Tennyson's privilege to carry it to the highest level it has yet reached.

Clumsy talk concerning poetry—not worthy to be called criticism—encourages people without ears for the music of verse, to admire profound thought in rugged expression all the more because of the ruggedness. Mellifluous expression is disdained; treated as only associated with shallow thinking. This is a very shallow view of the whole subject. The essential difference between prose and poetry depends upon form altogether. Vapid thinking clothed in harmonious language, expressed at all events in rhythmic if not in rhymed verse, however worthless, is poetry, though bad poetry. Thoughts, however noble and profound, expressed in language that disregards rhythm and sound, may be impressive and thrilling even, but do not constitute poetry. When thought and form are both beautiful we have good poetry.

Most of us feel, though few scientifically understand, the power of sound in connexion with language. Pope, in the "Essay on Criticism," partly suggests the idea:—

"When Ajax strives some rock's vast weight to throw
The line too labours and the words move slow.
Not so when swift Camilla scours the plain
Flies o'er the unbending corn and skims along the main."

In this illustration the first line "labours" simply because the words cannot be pronounced easily in rapid succession, while this is possible with the last two lines. But the power of sound is more subtle than the capacities of the tongue. Students of Nature's least familiar laws—occultists—are well aware of the potency of certain words and combinations of words in producing not merely emotion on the part of the hearer, but definite effects on elemental nature. "Mantrams," as such potent phrases are called, will give rise to what seem magical effects sometimes, in the physical world. Poetry does not aim at results of that order, but the Masters of the art know how to enlist the power of sound in appealing to emotion. And

Tennyson does this sometimes with startling effect. For instance, in "The Lady of Shalott," there are two verses that illustrate this art within art in a very striking manner. When the heroine of that beautiful allegory, tired of the mere visions of the world granted to her guarded seclusion, sees Lancelot riding past her island, the impression he gives her is described in a few lines in which the words by their mere sound, apart from their meaning, are exciting and exhilarating:—

"All in the blue unclouded weather
Thick jewelled shone the saddle leather.
The helmet and the helmet feather
Burn'd like one burning flame together,
　　As he rode down to Camelot."

Contrast those lines with another four which describe the dreary conditions prevailing when the heroine comes down to her boat and prepares to meet her death:—

"In the stormy east wind straining
The pale yellow woods were waning,
The broad stream in his banks complaining,
Heavily the low sky raining
　　Over tower'd Camelot."

Besides the mental picture the words evoke by their meaning, their sound is dismal and depressing.

I recognised this value of sound long before I intellectually understood it, for I knew "The Lady of Shalott" by heart as a boy—more years ago now than would constitute an ordinary life-time. But in these latter years I have learned from Tennyson himself that he is now, in his present inter-incarnate period, specially engaged in studying the deep inner meaning of sound as associated with uttered words. Last time he invested poetry with melodious beauty it had never reached before— with new and varied rhythms. Next time on these he will doubtless superadd appeals to emotion through sound in some way which we cannot yet foresee.

The "Memoir" here and there gives us interesting reminiscences of comments by Tennyson on his own poetry considered merely in reference to its artistic form. One such utterance shows us how he was already watchful of sound effects, independently of the ideas conveyed. "There are many other things besides, for instance, a fine ear for vowel sounds and the kicking of the goose out of the boat—(*i.e.*, doing away with sibilations).... I never, if possible, put two ' s's ' together in any verse of mine. My line is not, as first misprinted and often misquoted:—

>And freedom broadens slowly down

but

>And freedom slowly broadens down."

The hissing sound of the frequent s's is, of course, a great defect of the English language against which all careful writers, whether of verse or prose, have to be on their guard.

In "The Lotus Eaters" thought is so appropriately blended with sound that the mantric value of the sound is less apparent, but with attention one can trace this all through the poem, some parts of which may be taken as examples of the most perfect music in verse to be found in poetry up to the present time. The introductory verses illustrate something else as well—Tennyson's descriptive power. In a few words he frequently evokes mental pictures that flash upon the reader with surprise, like a scene suddenly revealed by lightning. Take, for example, almost any one of the introductory verses—the only verses in all Tennyson's writing that are Spenserian in their form. The fact that this is so, is interesting in itself. In his last life as Spenser he wrote the whole of "The Faerie Queene" in the well known metre also adopted by Byron in "Childe Harold." Why did not the habit cling to him? Certainly not because the metre is troublesome for the writer—with its quadruple rhyme in each stanza. He boldly grapples with quadruple rhyming in "The Lady of Shalott" and in some other poems. But in the former life he had already given the world the Spenser form. In this one he had to devise new forms of beauty. But see how easily when he likes he handles the old metre, with perception of the value of sound added to its rhythmic charm:—

"A land of streams! some like a downward smoke
Slow dropping veils of thinnest lawn did go.
And some through wavering lights and shadows broke,
Rolling a slumbrous sheet of foam below.
They saw the gleaming river seaward flow
From the inner land: far off three mountain tops
Three silent pinnacles of aged snow
Stood sunset flushed, and dew'd with showery drops,
Up-clomb the shadowy pine above the woven copse."

In the "Choric Song" which follows the introductory verses the elements of beauty are numerous and varied, the whole being dominated by the desire for "rest from weariness"—from the long labour of life:—

"But propt on beds of amaranth and moly
How sweet (while warm airs lull us blowing lowly)
With half dropt eyelid still
Beneath a Heaven dark and holy
To watch the long bright river drawing slowly
His waters from the purple hill.
To hear the dewy echoes calling
From cave to cave through the thick twined vine,
To watch the emerald colour'd water falling
Through many a woven acanthus wreath divine.
Only to hear and see the far off sparkling brine,
Only to hear were sweet stretched out beneath the pine."

Taking together both the sound of the words, and the vividness of the mental pictures they evoke, this fragment must merely be ranked *among* the most beautiful passages in poetry, though it would be impossible to select any one and declare it *the* most beautiful.

In "Locksley Hall" there is more strength and passion than in "The Lotos Eaters"—designedly dreamy and languid. The tenderness of the beginning dealing with the hero's recollections of Amy before losing her is in striking contrast with the greater part of the poem, which depicts his grief and anger. And there is one figure of speech in the earlier part with which the author himself is said to have been peculiarly pleased:—

"Love took up the harp of life and smote on all the
    chords with might,
Smote the chord of self which trembling, passed
    in music out of sight."

Needless to emphasise the general beauty of the whole poem. So many of its vivid phrases have passed into common use that like, "Hamlet," it may be described as full of quotations.

Still deferring consideration of the occult wisdom in the later works, it is well to take note of the way Tennyson is not merely a great poet, but a congeries of great poets. His complete works are generally grouped more or less in accordance with the order of their original publication, but a more significant classification would group them more or less in accordance with their character. Say as follows:—

1st.—The poems of beauty: "The Lady of Shalott," "The Lotos Eaters," "The Palace of Art," "Locksley Hall," "The Day Dream," and a score of others, but anyone wanting to understand Tennyson should begin by getting thoroughly familiar with the poems just named.

2nd.—The narrative poems: "The Princess," "Maud," "Enoch Arden," "Aylmer's Field," being the most important.

3rd.—The poems of Patriotism and Loyalty: Some addressed to Queen Victoria and the Prince Consort, the "Ode to the Duke of Wellington," "The Charge of the Light Brigade," and others.

4th.—"The Idylls of the King." These constitute a department of literature by themselves. They would have made a great literary name for the author had they stood alone as his only work.

5th.—The plays: "Queen Mary," "Harold," "Becket," and others. They were received with enthusiastic admiration on their appearance and some were very successfully produced on the stage. But this little volume has a main purpose in view which would not be served by an elaborate review of all the varied fruits of Tennyson's genius, so of the plays I shall have nothing further to say.

6th.—The occult poems: "The Ancient Sage," "By an Evolutionist," "The Making of Man,"

"Dawn," "Vastness," "The Mystic," "The Higher Pantheism."

With reference to the narrative poem "Aylmer's Field," it is worth while to note that its plot, as a story, is the most crude and elementary that the earliest fiction writers ever made use of. It is simply the-young-lovers-and-stern-father idea. And yet, in Tennyson's hands this familiar situation is so exquisitely treated that it brings tears to the eyes of imaginative readers.

And here I may pause to insert an explanation of peculiar interest that I had from Tennyson himself in the course of a recent "conversation," if I may use that term in reference to converse with a person who has "passed on" to consciousness on another plane. I had been giving a lecture (of which he had taken cognisance) on his occult knowledge, and had been letting myself go in regard to my admiration for his work generally. When I got an opportunity of converse with him shortly afterwards I said I would not repeat my lecture, but would prefer rather to deal with "the spots on the Sun," with bits of fault-finding. By-the-bye, I may here record another somewhat similar attempt made a long time previously. I had said that in all the enormous mass of his published works there was only one poem I did not like—namely, the sequel to "Locksley Hall," called "Locksley Hall Sixty Years After." It seemed to me to deal with the passionate and beautiful emotions of the earlier poem in a

TENNYSON, THE GENIUS

scornful and disparaging spirit, as though time would not only wear out, but discredit the love passion of youth. Tennyson's answer simply was:—"I regret that I wrote it." That put an end to further conversation on the subject. But the fact that Tennyson of the higher plane made the remark I have quoted, lends special interest to the following passage in the "Memoir" that relates to the poem in question:

"My father said that the old man in the second 'Locksley Hall,' had a stronger faith in God and in human goodness than he had had in his youth, but he had also endeavoured to give the moods of despondency which are caused by the decreased energy of life.

"His MS. note on the poem is—'a dramatic poem and dramatis personæ are imaginary. Since it is so much the fashion in these days to regard each poem and story, as a story of the poet's life or part of it. . . .'"

He goes on at some length to repudiate this notion. The "Memoir" tells us that four lines written for the first "Locksley Hall," but not included in the published poem, were the "nucleus" of the sequel. These are the lines:—

"In the hall there hangs a painting—Amy's arms about my neck,
Happy children in the sunshine sitting on the ribs of wreck.

In my life there was a picture—she that clasped
    my neck had flown,
I was left within the shadow, sitting on the wreck
    alone."

I fail to see how those lines can have been the nucleus of or suggestion for the later poem, which must have been prompted in some other way—by any one of the many incidents that show, or sometimes show, the decline of youthful emotions in later life.

The "Memoir" quotes a letter about the second "Locksley Hall" written to Miss Mary Anderson by Lord Lytton, which applauds the poem for a reason that has nothing to do with its main idea—disparagement of the emotion in its predecessor. Lord Lytton finds the second poem admirable because the first "furnished misunderstood and misapplied texts to a whole tribe of traders in silly and pernicious rubbish of neo-radicalism." The second, as Lord Lytton read it, repudiated all this. This criticism is an amusing illustration of the few lines in "The Day Dream" apropos to the demand of "Lady Flora" for a "moral" to that story:—

"For every man that walks the mead
    In bud or blade or bloom may find
According to his several need
    A meaning suited to his mind."

Coming back now to my "spots on the Sun," my first complaint had reference to a verse in "The

May Queen," when the dying girl gives her mother instructions about her burial:—

"You'll bury me, my mother, just beneath the hawthorn shade,
And you'll come sometimes and see me where I am lowly laid.
I shall not forget you, mother, I shall hear you when you pass
With your feet above my head in the long and pleasant grass."

This is an exasperating view to take of death—the mere undertaker's view—which multitudes of people have been condemned to by reason of the culpable and stupid ignorance of the clergy in regard to the real course of human life. They use phrases that imply a belief in some kind of existence beyond the grave, but these are so shadowy and unconvincing that they leave mourners a prey to miserable thoughts that link all memories of any beloved one departed with the discarded vehicle of life dealt with according to the ghastly fashions of the cemetery. But in so far as Tennyson's verse just quoted encourages a diseased habit of mind in regard to death, his answer to my protest was simply that at the time he wrote, in the first half of the nineteenth century, no view of death such as enlightened people hold now, could possibly have been understood. He could not help himself, he could merely embellish the prevailing view with such graceful fancies as it left room for. He seemed quite to agree with me that poetry in this respect must be reformed in future. There was no time to expand the conversation along that line of thought. It took another and very interesting course, as I will explain directly, but the time must come when poets dealing with death will dwell on the joyful conditions of existence on the happy levels of the Astral world, not on the gloom of the graveyard. For example, Moore in bidding "Farewell to Araby's daughter" at the end of the "Fireworshippers" ought to have turned his exquisite verses into a joyous welcome greeting her arrival in the Astral world.

My next "spot on the Sun" was a certain passage in "The Day Dream," as it is called in later editions, "The Sleeping Beauty," as it was called on its first appearance in "Poems Chiefly Lyrical" of 1830. This is one of my especial favourites among the poems of beauty, and has a tinge of occultism even, for consider the passage beginning:—

> "Well—were it not a pleasant thing
>   To fall asleep with all one's friends,
> To pass with all our social ties
>   To silence from the paths of men,
> And every hundred years to rise
>   And learn the world and sleep again."

That is simply a poetic sketch of the law of reincarnation. It recognises the way in which that law keeps people who care for one another together instead of dispersing them. But earlier in the poem Tennyson seems guilty of an inconsistency—of an offence against scientific truth with which all through his work he is generally in perfect harmony. He has told us that in the sleeping palace all activities of life are in suspense:—

"Here rests the sap within the leaf,
   Here stays the blood along the veins."

And those conditions are faithfully observed almost all through the poem. For instance, where the maid and page are interrupted in their little flirtation:—

"Her lips are sever'd as to speak,
   His own are pouted to a kiss,
 The blush is fix'd upon her cheek."

And yet we are told in regard to the enchanted Princess herself:—

"Year after year unto her feet,
   She lying on her couch alone
 Across the purple coverlet
   The maiden's jet black hair has grown."

Surely, I ventured to point out, you can't have it both ways. If processes of growth, according to the previous lines about the sap and the blood are absolutely suspended, hair would not grow whether you treat it as of the vegetable or animal kingdom, and there would have been no "full black ringlets downward roll'd" to enhance the beauty of "the perfect form in perfect rest."

Tennyson's answer was very interesting. He had himself been troubled by the apparent inconsistency, after having written the verses about the Princess in the way we know. He spent a week or ten days in trying to recast that part of the poem so as to avoid what seemed the mistake, but he was "balked"! That was the term he used. He felt himself somehow prevented (thus early half-conscious of higher powers guiding him) from altering the original form of the passage in question. And since "passing on" he has learned the reason. Human hair is a growth of a very peculiar order. It does not obey the ordinary laws either of vegetable or animal growth. Indeed, this idea is supported by the more or less well-known fact that hair continues to grow on a dead body—until this undergoes actual decay. So, if you begin by investing the Princess's body with continued existence free from natural decay for a hundred years, her hair actually would grow to the extravagant extent described in the poem. Far from being a scientific blemish, the description as it stands is scientifically accurate.

Perhaps the most interesting aspect of the little story I have just told lies in the fact that the poet was "balked" when he tried to alter his work as it stood. Inspiration is a process which occult study enables us to understand much better than in the loose fashion of commonplace thinkers. It is constantly going on in connexion with every kind of intellectual activity, in almost every kind of literary activity. And the sources of inspiration vary within very wide limits. In other words, some beings on higher planes of existence may be merely a little more advanced, a little better able to think than those they care about still in physical life. They may try to influence the thinking of their friends accordingly, and may have some little success or complete failure according to the receptivity or sensitiveness of the friends. Then, on the highest level of all, poetic thought may emanate from the sublime Master of poetry himself and may be directed to an Ego in incarnation (like Tennyson), himself sensitive to such influence in a perfect degree. In all cases the word "inspiration" fits the fact to be dealt with. It is quite unnecessary to surround it with any sacred character—though it *may* have a sublimely sacred origin. We might as well think of speech as something sacred in itself. It has been employed for supremely sacred purposes, but also by the worst criminals to promote crime in others.

Reverting now to my attempt to group Tennyson's poems into six categories, the reader will perceive that none of these include "In Memoriam," nor any of the northern dialect poems. Strangely enough, the general recognition of Tennyson as a very great poet dates from the publication of "In Memoriam." Now that we contemplate the complete works, it is the one work, important as regards its magnitude, that claims least attention. Certainly it includes passages of philosophical dignity, but is mainly an outburst of personal grief with which one can sympathise, but must find wearisome if he reads on steadily. As for the dialect poems, if they had never been written the world's debt to the writer would not have been lessened. Some people I know find them very charming and amusing, but they do not at present claim special attention from me.

While still concerned with the poems of genius (as distinct from those having occult significance) we may do well to observe how these very often have an inner meaning still within the area of thought relating to ordinary human emotion. The allegory in "The Lady of Shalott" is comparatively simple. The guarded unreal life of a girl in the upper class, hedged round with artificial restrictions, disqualifies her from facing great strong emotions in contact with a freer life. In "The Palace of Art" again we have an allegory too vivid to need interpretation. Purely selfish indulgence in pleasure of the senses, even of the higher senses, becomes a sin in excess, however innocent in moderation. The heroine of the poem (the human soul?), does not fall into the Puritanical blunder of wanting to destroy objects of beauty:—

"Yet pull not down my palace towers that are
  So lightly, beautifully built,
Perchance I may return with others there
  When I have purged my guilt."

In the little poem called "The Islet" we have to deal with a far more subtle suggestion, but still with one belonging to the category of human emotion and human duty. A happy bride is asking her new husband-lover where they shall go, "for a score of sweet little summers or so." He playfully asks, shall it be over the seas "to a sweet little Eden on earth I know," and proceeds to describe the lovely Islet in lines which are not merely exquisite in their form, but include a touch of poetic art worth notice for its own sake. In the middle of the description the metre changes. One might think that would jar upon the ear used to the flow of the normal metre, but instead of doing so the irregularity has a peculiarly beautiful effect. I quote a few of the regular lines and print the exceptional lines in italics to emphasise their effect:—

"Waves on a diamond shingle dash,
  Cataract brooks to the ocean run,
Fairily-delicate palaces shine
Mixt with myrtle and clad with vine,
And overstreamed and silvery streaked
With many a rivulet high against the sun,
The facets of the glorious mountain flash
Above the valleys of palm and pine."

The bride is, of course, eager to go there, but he says "No, no, no!"

"For in all that exquisite isle, my dear,
  There is but one bird with a musical throat;
  And his compass is but of a single note
  That makes it one weary to hear."

She says "Mock me not! Mock me not! Love, let us go," but he answers again, "No."

"For the bud ever breaks into bloom on the tree
  And a storm never wakes on the lonely sea,
  And a worm is there in the lonely wood
  That pierces the liver and blackens the blood
  And makes it a sorrow to be."

Now what is the bird with one note, and what is the worm in the wood? The bird, of course, is obvious. If the lovers seclude themselves in agreeable surroundings with nothing whatever to do or think about but their love for one another, they will in time be weary even of that beautiful emotion—but about the worm! I had discussed this question with a certain friend of mine and a suggestion had arisen. Lives spent, however innocently, in mere self-regarding enjoyment, out of touch with fellow creatures, uselessly from the point of view of the Divine purpose in humanity, would be stung at last with a perception of the way in which they had missed the loftier purposes of life. Such remorse would be misery.

I had an opportunity of asking Tennyson himself in the course of my recent studies of his work what he intended the worm to signify and he said, or in words to that effect: "Oh, merely the final culmination of the weariness of the lovers, with their one note." Then I told him what had been the idea developed by my friend, and he frankly declared: "I like that interpretation much better than my own!"

Inspiration is sometimes richer in significance than it seems on the surface, and at all events the case in point illustrates again the verse in "The Day Dream" about the varied "morals" to be evolved from the same story.

Someone, I think, once endeavoured to define genius as an infinite capacity for taking pains—which is really as misdirected a conception as that, on a level with it, which assigns psychic experiences at night to indigestion. But genius is compatible with taking pains, and the "Memoir" shows us how Tennyson was never weary of his work, adding to and developing his more important poems; sometimes, to an extent that many of us would deplore, applying the pruning knife.

CHAPTER III

TENNYSON, THE OCCULTIST

BEFORE entering on a systematic study of the Occultism imbedded in some of Tennyson's poems, it may be well to have a clear understanding with the reader as to the real meaning of the word "Occultism" in this connection. Sometimes it is taken to include all kinds of more or less undignified pursuits, fortune-telling in all varieties, ceremonial "magic" of an unhealthy order, the investigation of ghostly hauntings and so forth. In its loftier significance it means the study of Divine Wisdom; of the supreme truths underlying all the great religions of the world; of the laws governing human evolution; of the early history of this planet æons before events were recorded by any methods of writing. How are such studies to be carried on? Obviously, by no research dependent on written records of any kind. But though the majority, even of the cultured classes in civilised countries, are hardly aware of the fact—often wilfully blind to it—the relative minority, profiting by ever improving opportunities, are alive to the profoundly interesting truth that other senses beyond the familiar five open up avenues of information, of perception, of communication with levels of existence on which knowledge expands to an almost unlimited extent. With what will be regarded in the future as incomprehensible fatuity, guardians of narrow-minded orthodoxy—the crystallised ignorance of the past—try to warn off the leaders of thought from pursuing such lines of study, grotesquely pretending to know what we are "intended" to leave unknown.

On the other hand, confident in the conviction that if we *can* penetrate any given mystery of Nature, we must have been privileged by Divine decree to do so; perceiving also for a score of reasons that "we are ancients of the Earth, and in the morning of the Times," we who are devoted to the study of the higher occultism, "with open eyes desire the Truth," and within recent years have been bountifully assisted from the higher levels of existence to gain it in rich abundance. The conditions under which this has been done, and the expanded knowledge itself, have been described in full detail in books from my own pen and others, and that which is now the abundant literature of theosophy and the higher occultism, may easily be consulted by any readers of this volume who may wish to verify ideas and principles which are taken for granted at this moment, though elaborately set forth, examined and established elsewhere.

At present my purpose is to show that the superphysical knowledge thus acquired has enabled some of us to make the deeply interesting discovery that it must have been to a considerable extent already in Tennyson's possession when he wrote certain poems, and must have been underlying his thought in connexion with the creation of many others.

The world was not ripe for the higher occultism when he wrote, so instead of giving out definite teaching, as truth derived from exalted wisdom, he could only hint at it sometimes or disguise it as "a random arrow from the brain." In his later life, indeed, he ventures to be a little more explicit, and among the poems of that period, which are almost revelations, we may examine "The Ancient Sage" as—from one point of view—the most important. If that had never been written the future estimate of Tennyson would not have been quite what it will be when "newer knowledge moving nigh, brings truth that sways the souls of men." The utterances of the Sage are such as one might expect from an initiated Adept! The poem embodies a conversation between the Adept and a young friend who respects and admires him while himself being still an epicurean sceptic. He has written a poem inspired by that view of life, bits of which he reads to the Adept, who comments upon them. The young man reads from his scroll:—

> "But man to-day is fancy's fool
>   As man hath ever been,
> The nameless Power or Powers that rule
>   Were never heard or seen."

The Sage says:—

> "If thou would'st hear the Nameless and will dive
>   Into the Temple cave of thine own self
>   There, brooding by the central altar thou
>   May'st haply learn the Nameless hath a voice."

But though the Sage expands this idea, the young man's verses repeat the former complaint:—

> "But since—from when this earth began
>   The Nameless never came
> Among us—never spake with man
>   And never named the Name——"

The Sage interrupts:—

> "Thou can'st not prove the Nameless, O my son,
>   Nor can'st thou prove the world thou movest in.
>
> * * * * *
>
> Thou can'st not prove that I who speak with thee
>   Am not thyself in converse with thyself,
>   For nothing worthy proving can be proven
>   Nor yet disproven: therefore, be thou wise,
>   Cleave ever to the sunnier side of doubt,
>   And cling to Faith beyond the forms of Faith."

The Sage goes on expanding this idea, and then the verses strike a new note:—

"The years that make the stripling wise
  Undo their work again
And leave him, blind of heart and eyes,
  The last and least of men."

The dismal aspects of senility are effectively portrayed, for after all the verses, though intentionally representing false conceptions, are Tennyson's, and beautiful in form. The Sage's answer, too long to quote here in its entirety, expands the thought expressed in one line:—

"The doors of Night may be the gates of Light."

Then follows a passage of peculiar significance which puts on record an actual experience of his own that Tennyson refers to in notes left for his son to use in the "Memoir." He adopted a method of self-hypnotisation well-known to occultists, the effect of which, in the case of persons adequately qualified, is to set free the consciousness—the real Ego—from the trammels of physical life. The method is simple enough. The person concerned sits quiet and alone, and repeats his own name an enormous number of times till the sound seems to lose all definite meaning, and at last he finds himself out of the body—in the Astral body—conscious of what is commonly called the next world. If the experiment is successful, the person brings back into his waking remembrance the experiences, that may be far reaching and important, of his plunge into the higher life. The Sage describes his own experiences along these lines:—

" . . . for more than once, when I
Sat all alone revolving in myself
The word that is the symbol of myself
The mortal limit of the Self was loosed
And passed into the Nameless as a cloud
Melts into Heaven. I touched my limbs, the limbs
Were strange, not mine—and yet no shade of doubt
But utter clearness, and through loss of Self
The gain of such large life as matched with ours
Were Sun to spark—unshadowable in words
Themselves but shadows of a shadow world."

A very interesting confirmation of the fact that this passage reflected an actual experience of the author is to be found in the testimony of Professor Tyndall given—without a full realisation of its importance—in a paper of reminiscences supplied after the poet's death to his son and included in the "Memoir" which the "Son" ultimately published. Tyndall is describing a visit he paid to the poet at Farringford, and he writes:—

"With great earnestness Tennyson described to me a state of consciousness into which he could throw himself by thinking intently of his own name. It was impossible to give anything that could be called a description of the state, for language seemed incompetent to touch it. It was an apparent isolation of the spirit from the body. Wishing, doubtless, to impress upon me the reality of the phenomenon he exclaimed:—'By God Almighty there is no delusion in the matter. It is no nebulous ecstacy, but a state of transcendent wonder associated with absolute clearness of mind.'" Then Tyndall goes on with a few remarks that show his utter failure to appreciate the true significance of what Tennyson had told him. He says: "Other persons with powerful imaginations have had, I believe, similar experiences. Walking out with a friend one evening, the poet Wordsworth approached a gate and laying hold of its bars, turned to his companion and said: 'My dear sir, to assure myself of the existence of my own body, I am sometimes obliged to grasp an object like this and shake it.'" Of course, the attitude of Wordsworth's mind in saying this was ludicrously the reverse of Tennyson's, merely representing an effort to assure himself—as against the no-matter theory of Berkley—of the objectivity of matter. But at the same time Tyndall is perfectly honest in recording the Tennysonian view so far as he understood it. Further on in the paper from which I have already quoted, he refers to the passage above given in "The Ancient Sage." "On receipt of your request," he says, addressing the "Son," then preparing the "Memoir"—"I looked up the account of my first visit to Farringford and there, to my profound astonishment, I found described that experience of your father's which in the mouth of the Ancient Sage was made the ground of an important argument against materialism and in favour of personal immortality eight and twenty years afterwards.... If you turn to your father's account of the wonderful state of consciousness superinduced by thinking of his own name and compare it with the argument of the Ancient Sage, you will see that they refer to one and the same phenomenon."

Tyndall's view of the experience as simply an "argument" in favour of personal immortality is an amusing illustration of the extent to which the cultured world of his day was still quite unripe for occult teaching, at all events unripe to pick up the significance of hints in that direction. But we have been living, for the last 50 years, in a period of rapid transition from one stage of human development to another, and to many thousands of occult students now, the full meaning of Tennyson's achievement—as putting him in touch with the higher world of Knowledge concerning the Divine Hierarchy and our relations with it, will be vividly apparent.

The final passage of "The Ancient Sage" is a condensed epitome of the ethical teaching embodied in the Higher Occultism, with allusions to the meaning of the great initiations. The "weird casket" (occultism) holds merely a skull for the profane observer.

"But in the hand of what is more than man
Or in man's hand when man is more than man,"

TENNYSON, THE OCCULTIST

its contents are of another order. The last line is a plain allusion to the possibility that "man" may rise to the dignity of the Divine Hierarchy along the paths of the higher initiation.

Then the Sage gives his young friend a stream of moral injunctions identical in their significance with the lofty view of life to which all theosophical students are familiar—at all events in theory. The theory, in the language of indiscreet enthusiasm, often assumes fanatical exaggeration, but the Sage, though covering all the ground, is throughout alive to "the falsehood of extremes," he says:—

"Let be thy wail, and help thy fellowmen."

He does not even claim exclusive devotion to the service of others without a thought even of spiritual reward, but he warns the pupil not to

"—list for guerdon in the voice of men."

Again:—

"Nor roll thy viands on a luscious tongue."

He does not stoop to describe one kind of food rather than another as important to spiritual development, merely indicating that one should not seek pleasure in gluttony. The wisest occult principle in regard to eating and drinking simply tells us to find out what kind of food, etc., keeps the body in the best of health, and live accordingly. On this plane of life the body is the instrument by means of which we can do whatever work duty prescribes, and we ought to keep it in the best available working order. Then, in regard to the proper human attitude towards lower forms of life, the Sage again knows where to draw the line. We are not to:—

"—harm an adder through the lust for harm
  Nor make a snail's horn shrink for wantonness."

The delicately expressive language evades misconception. We may rightfully destroy—kill—noxious reptiles, but we should do this as a disagreeable duty. It is possible to exaggerate even to nonsense, the profound truth that killing any creature for the pleasure of the "sport" is a sin—of no great Karmic importance for the savage or even for the civilised man who has never glimpsed the higher law and is more or less a savage still in spite of his superficial polish; but the occultist who once reaches a comprehension of the true relation between humanity and the lower forms of life, and yet takes pleasure in defying the Divine purpose of evolution—in his case the "lust for harm" would become seriously prejudicial to his progress.

Then, having dealt with elementary morals, the Sage touches a more advanced idea:—

"And more—think well! Do well will follow
    thought."

Without interpretation this line, so curiously condensed, will perhaps be hardly intelligible; but it shows that the Sage (and, therefore, his creator, Tennyson) understood the deep significance of that sometimes puzzling occult teaching which gives right thought precedence over right action. Misunderstanding it, people sometimes fancy it means that it does not matter what you do, so long as you think correctly as to what you ought to do. The real meaning, of course, is that unless you get into the habit of thinking aright, as regards your duty in this life, you are apt to do wrong by inadvertence. As we go on with the study of Tennyson's poetry we shall find many other lines which show him conscious of profound truth for which the world in his day was hardly ready. Indeed, the few lines which conclude "The Ancient Sage" illustrate what has just been said. They are as follows:—

"—leave the hot swamp of voluptuousness
A cloud between the Nameless and thyself
And climb the Mount of Blessing whence, if thou
Look higher, then perchance—thou may'st, beyond
A hundred ever rising mountain lines
And past the range of Night and Shadow, see
The high heaven dawn of more than mortal day
Strike on the Mount of Vision."

The author of those lines had certainly a far more vivid conception of the heights and conditions to which "The Path" of initiation leads, than it was of any use to tell his readers in the middle of the last century.

That he himself had interior enlightenment in the matter as far back as the beginning of the century is shown by that curious poem "The Mystic" (to which brief reference has already been made), which was actually published among "Poems Chiefly Lyrical" in 1830. By some strange chance—not, as I have reason to believe, through any intention on the part of the author, it dropped out of later collections of his works, but can still be found in the early volume.

Theosophical readers will be interested in hearing that my attention was first drawn to "The Mystic" by a quotation from it made by the Master K. H. in a letter to me written apropos to the appearance of my first book, "The Occult World," in which I had endeavoured to describe the "Adept," the vague title by which we then spoke of the "Brothers" of the great "White Lodge." He wrote:—"You might have closed your book with these lines of Tennyson's:—

'How could ye know him? Ye were yet within
The narrower circle: he had well-nigh reached
The last which with a region of white flame
Pure, without heat, into a larger air
Upburning and an ether of black blue
Investeth and ingirds all other lives.' "

These are the concluding lines of the poem. It

TENNYSON, THE OCCULTIST

consists of forty-six lines, some of which defy exact interpretation, as, for example, these:—

> "Always there stood before him night and day
> Of wayward vary coloured circumstance
> The imperishable presence serene
> Colossal, without form, or sense, or sound,
> Dim shadows but unwaning presences,
> Four-faced to four corners of the sky."

"The Mystic" was published when the author was only 21, written no doubt at some earlier period. The obscurity of the lines just quoted may be due to the vague character of his inspirations at that date. It was not till his later life that his visions of occult truth were clear and detailed. But already at a very early period he had firmly grasped the idea of reincarnation. In the first of "The Early Sonnets" it is plainly set forth.

> "As when with downcast eyes we muse and brood
> And ebb into a former life. . . . .

> "So friend, when first I looked upon your face,
> Our thought gave answer each to each so true,
> Opposed mirrors each reflecting each,—
> That though I knew not in what time or place
> Methought that I had often met with you
> And either lived in either's heart and speech."

In "De Profundis" (an address to a newly-born child) the identity of the "spirit" with former manifestations is treated as a matter of course.

> ".... O dear spirit half lost
> In thine own shadow and this fleshly sign
> That thou art thou—who wailest being born
> And banished into mystery, and the pain
> Of this divisible-indivisible world....."

Then we have allusion to the "Infinite One."

> "Who made thee unconceivably Thyself
> Out of His whole World-self
> Live thou ....
> From death to death, thro' life and life and find
> Nearer and ever nearer Him who wrought
> Not Matter nor the finite infinite
> But this main miracle that thou art thou
> With power on thine own act and on the world."

There is far deeper thought and far deeper knowledge lurking in these purposely vague hints than can be read into Wordsworth's often quoted lines:—

> "Heaven lies about us in our infancy."

And—

> "Trailing clouds of glory do we come
> From God who is our home."

They are compatible with the idea that each new birth is due to a fresh emanation from the infinite divine consciousness, a new creation. And the probabilities are that Wordsworth worked with that thought in his mind when he wrote of "the soul that rises with us." Tennyson's conception

TENNYSON, THE OCCULTIST 59

of reincarnation was clear and distinct as even the sonnet shows, while later poems are unmistakable in the meaning. In one entitled, "By an Evolutionist," we find not merely the idea of reincarnation, but some of the latest teachings of advanced Theosophy condensed into a single verse. This little poem indeed is, in reference to the knowledge it shows, the most profoundly occult of any that even Tennyson ever wrote. It is included in the volume entitled "Demeter and other Poems," and the first verse gives us in four lines a complete summary of the method by which the growth of the Ego is accomplished. This is the verse:—

"The Lord let the house of a brute to the soul of a man
And the man said 'Am I your debtor?'
The Lord—'Not yet, but make it as clean as you can
And then I will let you a better.'"

Here we have in a nutshell the essence of Darwinism plus the illumination of the fundamental idea—the emergence of the human from the animal kingdom—by the clue which shows us the way in which the expansion of consciousness is provided for by the improvement of the vehicle in which it works. At first the occult student was inclined to regard the Darwinian view of evolution as leaving the part of Hamlet out of the play—as telling us nothing concerning the spiritual growth of the Ego within the gradually improving forms. Now we understand that mystery better. Consciousness is of only one kind, whether we think of it as working in the form of a guinea-pig, a sheep, a dog, a savage man, a civilised philosopher, a great Adept or Master of Wisdom, right up to any level we can think of in the Divine Hierarchy. The *efficiency* of the consciousness depends on the character of the vehicle or body in which it is active, and progress is accomplished by the effort the consciousness makes in any vehicle it inhabits for the moment to think beyond the limitations of that vehicle. We cannot easily realise the working of the principle at the vegetable or animal stage of the gradual process, but it is clearly intelligible when we are dealing with the human stage. If the man during an early human incarnation merely thinks of the physical interests of the moment, he drifts on into another life at the same level as the last, or very gradually, as incarnations follow one another, shares the slow upward pressure of the generations in which he finds himself, the evolutionary law for the multitude. But say, at any given life, he feels himself hampered by the limitations of his brain capacity. He makes efforts to which it does not adequately respond. In some line of mental or artistic activity he frets against the difficulty of realising the vague aspirations that he feels. He is making the best use of the vehicle he works in for the moment, but is discontented with the result. That discontentment ensures him an improved vehicle next time. Without as yet understanding the law, he has established a claim on Nature for an incarnation on a higher level. Obviously no one actually makes the best use of every capacity inherent in any current incarnation. If he did this he would ascend at a bound to much higher levels, but he makes definite progress along the line of the mental, artistic or moral activities which specially interest him and becomes greater in that respect. That is precisely the way in which men become great in science, art, literature, or philanthropy. They have made their "House"—or at all events some rooms in their house—"as clean as they can," and the Lord, in fulfilment of His promise, "lets" them a better.

There is a beautifully subtle meaning in the word "let" used in the verse quoted above. There is no finality in the transaction. Each successive incarnation is a temporary arrangement. The Lord does not "give"; He "lets" the body each time to the Ego, and the leases are of varying duration. Once we understand the law, it becomes glaringly obvious that Tennyson understood it when he wrote the lines quoted.

And the last verse of the poem shows that he could look beyond the growth of a Man as such to the infinitudes of spiritual progress for which human life is a preparation.

"I have climb'd to the snows of Age, and I gaze at a
	field in the Past
  Where I sank with the body at times in the
	sloughs of a low desire,
But I hear no yelp of the beast, and the Man is
	quiet at last
  As he stands on the heights of his life, with a
	glimpse of a height that is higher."

"The height that is higher" is, of course, the condition to be attained by means of the great initiations in the stupendous Divine Hierarchy, when all the opportunities that physical life can afford have been transcended, and the Ego has realised that progress beyond them is possible—even unto Infinity. Other poems, and especially "The Ancient Sage," may be richer in specific teaching concerning the earlier steps of the Path, but the few verses "By an Evolutionist" touch a far higher level of Wisdom, though this is so closely veiled that only in these latter days—when the author has passed to loftier regions of consciousness—can some of us, attaining to some of that wisdom by virtue of our own efforts at cleaning our houses, recognise the forecast that Tennyson left behind him for the benefit of a generation later than that which partially stifled even his prophetic genius.

A few verses called "The Making of Man" in the latest volume of new poems that he lived to publish are interesting as showing his grasp of the evolutionary idea, though less richly stored with inner meaning than the "Evolutionist." The ignorant misconceptions of human life and destiny on which conventional religious teachings are based are hopelessly misleading by reason of treating current humanity as a finality as far as this earth is concerned. Ecclesiastical doctrines, when confronted with their absurdity, take refuge in repudiation of their literal meaning. Even the resurrection of the body, though obviously grotesque nonsense in the literal sense, has been the subject of futile attempts to reconcile it with reason, but even such attempts convict it of assuming that a human being of our period is somehow stereotyped in eternity—polished up, perhaps, in other regions of existence, but him, or herself still. The fact that a man or woman of our time represents no more than a stage in the great creative undertaking that is improving humanity by degrees, is an elementary truth at the root of the higher knowledge hitherto occult, but dawning on cultivated understanding. Tennyson sets it forth in glowing language in the little poem already mentioned, "The Making of Man." Current humanity still bears traces of its origin—"moods of tiger or of ape"—but:—

"Man as yet is being made, and ere the crowning
   age of ages

Shall not æon after æon pass and touch him into shape?
All about him shadow still, but while the races flower and fade
Prophet eyes may catch a glory slowly gaining on the shade."

As usual in Tennyson's occultly inspired poems, the words all through show an inner meaning. The phrase above "while the races flower and fade" is clearly an allusion to the stages of evolution represented by the seven great root races, and the subraces of each. "Races" for the occultist have a much deeper signification than the modern ethnologist has as yet suspected. It is easy to guess—and some of us think we know—that Tennyson had visions that were not merely due to the imagination of poetic genius, but specific revelations of natural truth as definite as the teaching of established science, though touching regions of knowledge beyond the reach of ordinary scientific methods.

A brilliant bit of evidence to this effect may be found in one poem to which one would not naturally turn in search of occult hints, "The Charge of the Heavy Brigade at Balaclava"—not to be confused with the more familiar "Charge of the Light Brigade." It is all about flashing sabres and galloping troops and the glory of victorious combat. But it has an Epilogue. An imaginary critic* is supposed to have condemned the verses for glorifying the brutalities of warfare. But the poet answers to the effect that attacked by evil force we must resist by force. He who loves War for War's own sake, is fool, or crazed, or worse:—

"But since our mortal shadow—Ill
   To waste this world began—
Perchance through some abuse of will
   In worlds before the Man—
Involving ours—he needs must fight
   To make true peace his own.
He needs must combat might with might
   Or Might would rule alone—"

Many thousands must have read those lines without a glimmering suspicion of the fact that they reveal Tennyson in possession of the awful story of Satan's rebellion. No one could see their inner meaning without having had that story from teachers of more than ordinary human knowledge —as some of us have received it in recent years. In full detail it is more than need be repeated here, and ecclesiastical teaching concerning "The Devil" has made such ghastly nonsense of the whole subject that cultivated thought has been turned into the wrong direction in dealing with attempts to account for the origin of evil. The notion of

---

*The "Memoir" explains that the "imaginary critic" of the epilogue was in fact a real person—Miss Laura Tennant (the late Mrs. Alfred Lyttleton)—who put forward her objection to the poem in the course of a conversation with Tennyson on board a yacht.

focusing that on any spiritual individuality has been put aside as superstition. But the occultist knows but too well that there has been, during the whole life of this world, a Great Being at war with the Divine programme not merely of this world, but of the whole Solar System; that he (one must use some sort of pronoun) was not always at enmity with God, but rose to great heights of spiritual dignity by legitimate achievement—and at last through an appalling "abuse of Will in worlds before the man," before this earth was as yet in existence—undertook the stupendous task of warring against the Divine plan. Thus from the very beginning of humanity on earth, Satan, "our mortal shadow—Ill," has been striving to destroy humanity—"to waste this world" in the most thorough-going way imaginable.

Tennyson has told me that once when out of the body he was shown—in what the occultist technically calls "the Akasic records" the actual "breaking up of Satan's world." His use of this phrase showed me in a flash that he had been made acquainted with the whole wonderful story of the Satanic rebellion. This has never yet been told in print, and this is not an opportunity for breaking down the reserve which has enshrouded it, but the "asteroids," as they are called by astronomers, circulating between the orbits of Mars and Jupiter, are the fragments of the broken world to which Tennyson referred.

The thrilling vision in question was given him at the same time as a long series of others, illustrating in a more or less symbolical fashion the tumultuous history of the human race. Deeply impressed by these, on the day after he was given them at night, he wrote the poem called "Vastness," which must thus be included in the occult series, though not so definitely the fruit of occult teaching as the "Sage" or the "Evolutionist." Almost every verse embodies a contrast, grimly suggestive of the war in this world, between Good and Evil.

"Stately purposes, valour in battle, glorious annals of army and fleet,
Death for the right cause, death for the wrong cause, trumpets of victory, groans of defeat.

* * * * *

What the philosophies, all the sciences, poesy, varying voices of prayer
All that is noblest, all that is basest, all that is filthy with all that is fair."

But the final touch, suddenly bringing the personal note, proclaims belief in the future:—

"What is it all, if we all of us end but in being our own corpse-coffins at last
Swallowed in vastness, lost in silence, drowned in the deeps of a meaningless past.
What but a murmur of gnats in the gloom or a moment's anger of bees in their hive

Peace, let it be, for I loved him, and love him for ever; the dead are not dead but alive."

Although the author of the "Memoir" fails to discern the inner meaning of the occult allusions in the later poems, he evidently feels that they have a meaning of a more or less subtle kind. Concerning "By an Evolutionist" he says:—

"In the poem 'By an Evolutionist,' written in 1888 when he was dangerously ill, he defined his position; he conceived that the further science progressed, the more the Unity of Nature and the purpose hidden behind the cosmic process of matter in motion and changing forms of life would be apparent."

That is, of course, a poor guess at the meaning of the verses, but it is interesting to know that they were written when the author was dangerously ill —perhaps expecting, certainly without anxiety, an immediate transfer to those regions of life with which, during his excursions out of the body he had become familiar. He may have wanted to put on record a little more plainly than had been done up to that time the fact that he knew certain great truths surely destined to ultimate discovery.

The "Memoir" is emphatic in affirming his trust in the reality of the future life, but fails to appreciate the meaning of passages in the poems which mingle with belief in future life a perception of the future of evolution—I quote from the "Memoir."

"In 'Maud' he spoke of the making of man—

'As nine months go to the shaping an infant ripe for his birth
So many a million of ages have gone to the making of Man.
He now is first; but is he the last?'"

This is only one of innumerable hints he gives to explain that future life includes future activities on this physical plane of life. He did not find the mentally oppressive period we call the Victorian Age ready for open denunciation of the clumsy doctrines that contented the churches and the clergy, but he could forecast a time when, in the words of the "Memoir," "Christianity without bigotry will triumph, when the controversies of creeds shall have vanished and

' Shall bear false witness each of each no more
But find their limits by that larger light
And overstep them, moving easily
Through after ages in the Love of Truth
The Truth of Love.'"

These lines are a quotation from "Akbar's Dream." The poem entitled "The Higher Pantheism" was written in 1869 as a contribution to the discussions of a certain "Metaphysical Society" which Tennyson may be said to have founded—as its formation followed on a suggestion of his pointing to the desirability of having a Society or Club, embracing all varieties of Christian religion, for the discussion of Christian evidences. That is the account of its origin which we get in the "Memoir." Apparently for its first meeting Tennyson sent the poem which is hardly to be regarded as inspired by occult teaching, but, nevertheless, reflects some occult truths. We read:—

"The sun, the moon, the stars, the hills and the plains
Are not these, O Soul, the Vision of Him who reigns?
Is not the Vision He? though He be not that which He seems
Dreams are true while they last, and we do not live in dreams?"

True occult science includes this idea, though, of course, with the further idea that God is not lost in his Vision, but just as complete after accomplishing the work of creation as before.

Probably Tennyson intentionally refrained from putting any deep occult meaning into "The Higher Pantheism." The "Metaphysical Society" was not destined to bring about any important results, and however far in 1869 Tennyson may have been occultly illuminated, the group which constituted the Society would have been all the more obviously ill-fitted to appreciate a new revelation, because of the social, intellectual and ecclesiastical dignity of its members. Bishops and Deans were numerous—others of a type representing views of intense rigidity, Bagehot, Froude, Gladstone, James Martineau, would have been as little approachable with new thought out of tune with the century. In the "Memoir" we read:—

"The last meeting of the Society was held at Dr. Martineau's house on May 16, 1880. Huxley asserted that it died of 'too much love.' My father declared that it perished because after ten years of strenuous effort no one had succeeded in even defining the term 'Metaphysics.'"

This was a very suggestive remark. In the hands of all nineteenth century writers concerned with what they called "metaphysics" speculation was merely engaged in treating *thought* as in itself a subject for analysis. They utterly failed to understand that there are regions of natural phenomena outside and beyond the physical plane that are just as real, just as material in a lofty sense, just as completely independent for their existence on *human* thinking as the mountains and seas perceptible to the physical senses. There may be—doubtless there is—a kind of thought, that of God, which brings the mountains and seas into objective existence, but metaphysicians of the bygone type were blundering along a wrong road when (some of them) attributed or sought to attribute such phenomena to human thinking. A true science of metaphysics must deal with natural phenomena entirely beyond the range of the physical senses—with the view of Nature which occultism endeavours to obtain. Indeed, true "metaphysics" and "occultism" are convertible terms. That is what Tennyson perceived and that is the idea he must have had in his mind when making the remark quoted above.

The poem called "The Dawn" belongs clearly to the occult series. It emphasises the idea that the future destinies of Man are linked for æons to come with the life of this Earth. Conventional religious teaching has missed this all-important idea, and has thus made nonsense of immortality. There will come a time, certainly, when for each of us the experience to be gathered by lives on the physical plane will be complete. Then further progress in the direction of infinity will be accomplished by existence entirely spent on higher planes, but that kind of progress can only be begun when the earlier kind has been accomplished, and that can only be thought of as accomplished when on this earth æon after æon has moulded us into shape—when the processes of evolution we are going through shall have carried us to conditions as far superior to those of the ordinary man of to-day as that condition is superior to those of the tiger and the ape. People who fancy they can begin the higher non-physical progress from the stage at which they at present stand would be

TENNYSON, THE OCCULTIST 73

paralleled by anyone having to make a journey from London to Paris—to suggest a very crude illustration—who should say: "The part of the journey from London to Dover and Calais bores me: I will begin my journey from Calais." He can't do that without getting there first.

The first verse of "The Dawn" refers to the tiger and ape stage:—

"Screams of a babe in the red hot palms of a Moloch of Tyre,
　Man with his brotherless dinner on man in the tropical wood,
　Priests in the name of the Lord passing souls through fire to the fire
　　Head hunters and boats of Dahomey that float upon human blood."

A little further on the poem asks: "Is it shame so few should have climbed from the dens in the level below?" and the last verse answers:—

"Is it turning a fainter red? So be it, but when shall we lay
　The Ghost of the Brute that is walking and haunting us yet and be free
　In a hundred, a thousand winters? Oh, what will our children be
　The men of a hundred thousand—a million—summers away?"

Certainly a great many of Tennyson's simpler poems merely emphasise belief in the continuity of life beyond the grave, and the commonplace reader fails to see the occult significance of others, like "The Dawn," just quoted, that recognise the real laws of human growth—those that include an earthly programme for each of us in turn that provides time and opportunity for that earlier stage of the mighty journey, which will eventually lead us up to the level of the Divine Hierarchy.

In another short poem of the occult series, called "The Dreamer," we find "a Voice of the Earth" making piteous moan over the condition of the life that the Earth bears. It plainly suggests that Tennyson, in his touch with lofty teachers, had caught a glimpse of the way in which the planet itself—apart from the life it bears—has a life and consciousness of its own—or, more correctly, is animated by a Being of exalted consciousness. The Spirit of the Earth is a definite Being of a very lofty order—incapable, for that matter, of impatience with natural conditions of any kind, but in the poem it is supposed to bewail the loss of earlier visions:—

"And I clash with an iron Truth
When I make for an age of Gold,
For teeming with liars and madness and knaves
And wearied of Autocrats, Anarchs and Slaves
And darkened with doubts of a Faith that saves,
And crimson with battle and hollow with graves,
To the wail of my winds and the moan of my waves
I whirl and I follow the sun"—

The answer is summed up in the last verse:—

"For moans will have grown sphere music
 Or ever your race be run
And all's well that ends well
 Whirl and follow the sun."

True occult science and philosophy is profoundly optimistic as regards the ultimate future. That does not mean that it recommends an attitude of apathetic indifference to evil conditions operative at any given time. These have to be combated as they arise, but it is certain that among the multitudes of mankind, some will combat them— Free-will harmonises with Destiny when this idea is properly taken into account. For example, we find in the "Memoir"—without surprise—that Tennyson had a profound horror of Vivisection— a natural result of his touch with the Elder Brethren of mankind, already belonging to the great Divine Hierarchy. Besides those so in touch, there are, of course, large numbers of the more intellectually human representatives of ordinary mankind who share that horror; but it may safely be affirmed that no one can be in relations with the Divine Hierarchy without loathing the practice of vivisection in all its varieties. Concerning Tennyson's feeling on the subject, the "Memoir," referring to a conversation between Tennyson and Lord Napier of Magdala, says:—

"They then touched on Vivisection, my father

expressing his conviction that without anæsthetics no animal should be cut open for the sake of science. 'I have been reading,' he said, 'of the horrible and brutal experiments in Italy and France, and my whole heart goes out to a certain writer in the *Spectator* who declared he had yet to find out mankind was worth the cruel torture of a single dumb animal.' "

Now, of course, there are many very well-meaning people who attach so much importance to human life that any sacrifice of animal life—even if it includes animal suffering—seems relatively unimportant. They do not see how to get rid of the necessity for painless experiments on animals if all is to be done that can be done for the preservation of human life. How is the difficulty to be overcome? First, the preservation of any given human life beyond what may be thought of as its normal Karmic period is seen—from the point of view arising from a proper understanding of Reincarnation—to be less important than the pro-Vivisection thinker imagines, while the proper understanding of the true duty of humanity to the animal kingdom shows this to be enormously more important than such thinkers imagine. Thus, really the practice of Vivisection is an evil to be stamped out, as a necessary step in the moral progress of mankind at large. That will certainly be done as the truer view gains more and more adherents, but that can only be brought about by effort on the part of the most enlightened. The ultimate result is certain, because it is certain that the most enlightened will continue to make the effort. Free-will, uncertain in each individual case, is thus reconciled with the optimism I began by speaking of as inherent in true occult philosophy.

There is a passing, but very significant allusion to Vivisection in "The Princess," when the heroine of that charming story is conversing with the disguised Prince. He says—referring to the many schools within the feminine university:—

"Methinks I have not found among them all
  One anatomie."

The Princess answers:—

"'Nay, we thought of that,'
She answered, 'but it pleased us not in truth
We shudder but to dream our maids should ape
Those monstrous males that carve the living
  hound
And cram him with the fragments of the grave,'"

We need not always assume that ideas expressed by the dramatis personæ of his narrative poems are the poet's own ideas, but the words just quoted coupled with the Napier conversation, show that in this case they are.

In dealing with the utterances of an occultist like Tennyson, it is not easy to draw the boundary line between intelligent thinking of the ordinary physical-brain order and inspiration. And an account in the "Memoir" of his "talk" roughly noted down in 1887, so much seems prophetic—read in the light of later events—that the difficulty in question is enhanced. He said:—

"When I see Society vicious and the poor starving in great cities, I feel that it is a wave of evil passing over the world, but that there will be yet some new and strange development which I shall not live to see.... You must not be surprised at anything that comes to pass in the next fifty years. All ages are ages of transition, but this is an awful moment of transition."

This should not be read as a prophecy of the great war. The war, though perhaps rendered possible just when it took place by the transition period, was not in the Divine programme, but a fruit of Satanic activity, antagonising the Divine programme—correctly assigned to its real origin by the words:—

"But when our mortal shadow—Ill
To waste this world began—"

The transition period, as more definite occult teaching has shown, is that which inaugurates the new subrace—the sixth—of the great fifth root race. At all such periods social disturbance seems to be inevitable and that, setting in after the close of the war, as we came fully to realise in the year

1919, was the crisis that Tennyson foretold in 1887.

And a little further on in the "talk" recorded in the "Memoir," there is a brief hint that may ultimately be seen to have a prophetic value, though pointing to a period still in the future:—

"What we have to bear in mind is that even in a Republic there must be a guiding hand. Men of education, experience, weight and wisdom must continue to come forward. They who will not be ruled by the rudder will, in the end, be ruled by the rock."

We need not assume that Tennyson, in his physical waking consciousness, possessed a complete knowledge in detail of the super-physical information that has accumulated on our hands during the progress of the Theosophical Movement. Incarnate life has been described as "imprisonment in the five senses." Thus any given Ego may be in one condition of consciousness while so imprisoned; in quite another condition when set free from that even for the brief periods of sound sleep. And recollections of the higher conditions are drawn back into the waking state with more or less success according to the stage of evolution reached. Most of us do not bring back any such recollection at all; very few with complete detail; none quite completely, because there are levels of consciousness that may be reached by advanced Egos out of the body during sleep, which are so unlike those of the waking life that they cannot be focused on that life at all. In Tennyson's case his poetry shows that he knew a good deal more than he could give out at the period during which he wrote. The allusion to Satan quoted already could only have been written by one who knew the leading facts connected with the great rebellion. And the constantly-repeated allusions to the renewal of each life—reincarnation—and the evolutionary purpose to be fulfilled by the law, indicate a grasp of that group of natural truths which must have been fairly complete. The occult allusions in question are certainly few and far between, if we compare the poems that contain them with the marvellous range of those which deal with the emotions of ordinary human life. Those are the fruit of his accumulated genius which have long established him in the estimation of his devotees as the greatest poet who has lived amongst us as yet. But the charm of the earlier poems of beauty (according to my classification), of the narrative poems and of the Idylls will be all the more impressive when we recognise that their author, besides being the greatest poet—perhaps as one consequence of being that—was also, though more or less for obvious reasons in disguise, a herald of the greatest revelation of superphysical truth that has yet been given to the world.

That last remark claims some further elucidation and may excuse me for reiterating an explanation already given. Tennyson became "the Occultist," *because*, in the first instance, he became "the Genius." It was impossible that he could grow, from life to life in the past, along the line of development he had chosen, without in his inter-incarnate periods coming into touch with those great spiritual teachers whom occultists recognise as "Masters of Divine Wisdom." They have developed through many ages along the comprehensive lines of progress leading directly to identification with the Divine Hierarchy. They become agents of Divinity in the management of the world. It would thus have become possible for the Ego, which assumed the aspect we call Tennyson, to have merged his development before that stage in the developments leading towards the condition of Mastership. In this connexion we have to contemplate alternatives that may, perhaps, be better understood if we turn attention for the moment to the progress of that kind of genius directed towards scientific perfection. An Ego, who, life after life, through many thousands of years, devotes himself on earth to the study of the laws governing matter, becomes eventually what we commonly call a great scientist. *His* greatness in that line of development must assuredly, in all cases, put him in touch during inter-incarnate periods with the Masters of Wisdom. It would be open to him to forsake the work he had so far been concerned with, and follow in their footsteps through a course of initiation leading to their condition. Now that is undoubtedly the loftiest ambition by which any human being can be guided, but in some cases its fruition may be postponed for adequate reasons. Thus the great scientist, naturally finding himself on high planes of consciousness after his last important life on the physical plane, may see that he might carry on and develop further his last life's work by simply going on with scientific study on the higher planes. He knows quite well that the scientific *knowledge* he may thus acquire will not cling to his memory in the next life, but he knows equally well, that the intellectual *capacity* to acquire it in the next life will assuredly be his. Thus, for example, take the case of Sir Isaac Newton. He, as the usual phrase goes, discovered the law of gravitation in his last life. But he did not discover the method of its operation, and that has remained a mystery for every man of science ever since. By postponing for the present all further "*spiritual*" progress he is enabled to prepare himself for the *discovery* of the way in which the law of gravitation works when he returns to ordinary earth life next time. So that, as a matter of fact, within my own knowledge (to all intents and purposes) is exactly the way in which Newton is at present engaged. By following that course he regards himself—and no doubt is perfectly right in so thinking—as contributing to the progress of humanity better than he could do by prematurely forsaking the path of his own progress in pursuit of a lofty spiritual ideal. And I may add that his example is being followed—or a course of action similar to his is being pursued—by all the men who have been conspicuous in science during the last century.

Now, with appropriate modifications, the same course is being pursued by Tennyson. His progress—as a genius in his way—puts him in a position, amongst the great Masters of Wisdom, that would have enabled him to forsake the poetical career and enter at once on the progress leading towards that condition. He has chosen to follow out still further the beautiful task to which he has been devoted for so many recent lives. He will come back to incarnation, probably within the current century, and be a greater poet than ever. He is—he has told me—making a special study of the mantric value of sound in poetry, as I have already declared in discussing the sound effects produced by some verses in "The Lady of Shalott," without, at the time, plunging more deeply into the subject. I will attempt this now, but the effort claims some preliminary explanation.

Tennyson has very sublime assistance in his study of Sound as an element of beauty in verse. For one thing, he is in touch, of course, with the semi-Divine "Master," who presides over the art of poetry. The great expansion of our occult knowledge in recent years has, amongst other important new ideas, enabled us to understand that there are great Masters who specialise in the varied tasks connected with the progress of human evolution. Thus there is one at the head, so to speak, of all scientific progress. The Scientific Master is the inspirer of all scientific discovery, curbing it if it threatens to outrun the stage of knowledge to which, at any given period, the race then in activity is entitled; helping it forward, if some leap forward is appropriate to the period reached. When such a leap is due, the Scientific Master generally illuminates more than one mind with the new idea. This is the explanation of the fact often noticed that more than one of the great discoveries —the discovery of the undulatory theory of light is an example—seem to be made simultaneously by men of science in different countries. In connexion with poetry the same explanation holds good, though the operation of the system is less obvious. Is the first-rate poetical faculty less frequently found than the scientific? I am not prepared to say, but, anyhow, every great poet is in a certain sense a pupil of the Poetry Master, and Tennyson, I venture to think, a prize pupil.

The state of things I have just described is an illustration of the way in which Divine power works through varied channels or agencies. This is a deeply impressive result of our current enlightenment in reference to the sublime mysteries of the world's government. The fact that every department of human progress is presided over by an appropriately qualified Chief (the arts of music and painting have each their own), is merely a detail of the mighty truth. Apart from the cultivation of humanity, which may be regarded as the main purpose for which this world exists, the physical earth itself has to go through processes of growth corresponding to, and in a measure subservient to the gradual elevation of humanity towards its ultimate destinies. (As Tennyson was well aware, we are little more than half-way through the long journey in the direction of those destinies. "We are ancients of the earth, and in the morning of the times.") The growth of the earth itself, considered independently of the life it bears, is a stupendous department of Divine activity with its own chiefs and hierarchy. The recognition of this does not conflict with the simplest religious conception of the omnipotence and omnipresence of God. Travelling upward in thought, God is the synthesis of all the Divine agencies working in different departments; or, if we prefer to try and think first of God and then of His agencies, *they* are partial reflections of Himself.

Again, is the gradual improvement of animated form due merely to "natural selection"—a blind law of animal passion? That may be used as a force for bringing about some results, but the adaptation of animated forms to the advancing aspiration of incarnate consciousness is guided from on High, by Beings of Divine nature, as specifically as progress in Science and Art by other Beings of (only relatively) inferior degree. From the point of view of the enlightened occultist the crude shadowy conceptions of Divinity that have passed for religious beliefs all through the Middle Ages and satisfy an innocent multitude still, are the babbling of childhood compared with the sublimation of truth. And yet—"till newer knowledge moving nigh, brings truth that sways the soul of men"—they give rise to beautiful human character in many cases, as well as to foul bigotry. Creeds are often so offensive to clear understanding that when they do not poison spiritual emotion, but on the contrary seem to breed saints, fruit of that kind seems indeed a miraculous growth. But in the light of the Higher Wisdom it becomes partly intelligible. Divine influences, pouring on mankind through many channels, are more subtle than explicit language. The soaring aspiration of the truly religious devotee is itself exempt from the disguise of language. The response that it invokes is clothed in a finer vehicle than speech. And so the spirituality of the world has survived its conventional religion. But we are not doomed to depend for ever on the search for God, on mere inarticulate emotion. The higher occultism may for long—measuring intervals not by time, but by spiritual development—be still a search in the direction of infinitude, but, compared with the mental condition from which it escapes, is as the summit of a mountain to the depth of a mine. The paths leading up the mountain have been pointed out and explored. They were mysterious as a maze till recently; only known to a few climbers of rare attainment, but the days of difficulty are over, and the ascent is becoming possible for multitudes. For whom the signs on the way left to help them by those who passed on in bygone times are brightly interesting as we recognise them, and that is the explanation of the charm to be found in the occultism of Tennyson's poetry.

So now, after a long but inevitable digression, I may return to the special direction, or one special direction, that his present studies on higher planes of existence are now taking. Sound is a far more potent force than the science of our time has yet enabled us to understand. It is intimately associated with creative power. It is one of the means by which Divine Thought is thrown into manifestation, and as a natural collateral fact it is worked through an appropriate Divine Agency, as usual, of course, plus an appropriate subordinate hierarchy. To understand that last remark properly, it would be necessary to study those branches of Occultism relating to Elementals and Devas. But, anyhow, there is a sublime Chief at the head of the superphysical laws relating to the creative power of Sound, and it is in touch with that great Being that Tennyson is preparing himself in his next incarnation to use the power of Sound in words as evoking human emotion with an effect that even the poetry of his last life has but imperfectly foreshadowed.

For his next coming the world will not have to wait very long as worlds measure time. The current century is, in a much deeper sense than the term has been applied to the Nineteenth, a "wonderful" century. The awful catastrophes by which it has been inaugurated are infinitely more wonderful than most of us who have passed through them realise. The Satanic attack to which they have been due was unprecedented in the experience of spiritual observers on levels of existence commanding views over regions of manifestation within which our Solar System plays only a relatively small part. When, within the years that children now amongst us will live to see, the effects of that stupendous attack will have been obliterated, this world will enter on conditions that will indeed be Utopian compared to those around us at the moment. Very great Egos—on a far higher level than even our illustrious poet—will be taking form on Earth to guide an improved civilisation, and they will not be unattended. Not only will the long-rigid barriers between the physical and superphysical states of consciousness, already cracking in all directions, be broken down, but the advanced leaders of human progress, whose mere existence on higher planes was unsuspected by the metaphysician of the expiring generation, will be amongst us and recognised. In those days, with Tennyson and companions in other departments of genius as well, again incarnate amongst us, the readers of his future poetry will be themselves for the most part sufficiently developed to need no help in discerning his connexion with those regions of knowledge occult for mankind at large, and only ceasing to be so for a few as yet. But every step made in each life in the direction of higher knowledge bears important fruit in the next following incarnation, so the little expansion of thought which these humble efforts of mine may evoke for some of my readers will perhaps be the beginning of development that will mean more for them than the mere interest of the discovery that Tennyson in the life last passed was already an Occultist.

THE PELICAN PRESS

2 CARMELITE STREET